Henry Ford

by Lola M. Schaefer

Consulting Editor: Gail Saunders-Smith, Ph.D.

Consultant: Howard R. Pletcher, Researcher,
National Automotive and Truck
Museum of the United States,
Auburn, Indiana

Pebble Books

an imprint of Capstone Press
Mankato, Minnesota

Pebble Books are published by Capstone Press
151 Good Counsel Drive, P.O. Box 669, Mankato, Minnesota 56002
http://www.capstone-press.com

1 2 3 4 5 6 05 04 03 02 01 00

Library of Congress Cataloging-in-Publication Data
Schaefer, Lola M., 1950–
 Henry Ford/by Lola M. Schaefer.
 p. cm.—(Famous people in transportation)
 Includes bibliographical references and index.
 Summary: A brief biography of the man whose Model T automobile made the
gasoline-powered car affordable to Americans.
 ISBN 0-7368-0546-X
 1. Ford, Henry, 1863–1947—Juvenile literature. 2. Automobile industry and
trade—United States—Biography—Juvenile literature. 3. Industrialists—United
States—Biography—Juvenile literature. [1. Ford, Henry, 1863–1947. 2. Automobile
industry and trade—Biography. 3. Industrialists.] I. Title. II. Series.
TL140.F6 S33   2000
338.7′6292′092—dc21
[B]   99-047366

Note to Parents and Teachers

The series Famous People in Transportation supports national social studies standards related to the ways technology has changed people's lives. This book describes the life of Henry Ford and illustrates his contributions to transportation. The photographs support early readers in understanding the text. This book also introduces early readers to subject-specific vocabulary words, which are defined in the Words to Know section. Early readers may need assistance to read some words and to use the Table of Contents, Words to Know, Read More, Internet Sites, and Index/Word List sections of the book.

Table of Contents

Young Henry Ford 5

Plans and Inventions. 9

Ford Motor Company. 13

Words to Know 22

Read More 23

Internet Sites. 23

Index/Word List. 24

4

Henry Ford was born on a farm in Michigan in 1863. Henry liked to take apart farm machines. He wanted to learn how the machines worked.

Henry moved to Detroit
when he was 17 years old.
He learned about engines.
Henry had an idea for a
better gasoline engine.

Henry met Clara Bryant.
She believed in his ideas.
Henry and Clara married
in 1888. Henry worked
many hours in a workshop
behind their home.

Henry built a small gasoline engine to power a car. He built his first car in 1896. Henry called it the Quadricycle.

Henry began a car factory in 1903. He called it the Ford Motor Company. Workers made Model A cars at the factory.

14

Henry wanted to build a car that everyone could buy. The Ford Motor Company began to make Model T cars in 1908. Many people bought them.

Soon Henry owned the biggest car factory in the world. Henry worked to make cars faster and safer.

Henry began to use an assembly line in his factory. A moving belt brought cars to the workers. Each worker added one part to each car. The factory could make many cars with an assembly line.

Henry Ford died in 1947. His ideas changed how people made cars. Today, Henry's company still makes cars.

Words to Know

assembly line—an arrangement of workers in a factory; work passes from one person to the next person until the job is done; moving belts bring cars and car parts to assembly line workers at car factories.

engine—a machine that makes the power needed to move something; a car engine changes the energy in gasoline into the power needed to move the car.

factory—a building in which people and machines make items

gasoline—a liquid fuel made from oil; many cars use gasoline.

machine—a tool made of moving parts that is used to do a job

Gourley, Catherine. *Wheels of Time: A Biography of Henry Ford.* Brookfield, Conn.: Millbrook Press, 1997.

Joseph, Paul. *Henry Ford.* Checkerboard Biography Library. Minneapolis: Abdo & Daughters, 1997.

Middleton, Haydn. *Henry Ford: The People's Carmaker.* What's Their Story? New York: Oxford University Press, 1997.

Henry Ford Museum and Greenfield Village
http://www.hfmgv.org/index.html

International Motorsports Hall of Fame Member Henry Ford
http://www.historyonwheels.com/halloffame/1993/Henry_Ford_main.htm

The Model T Ford Club
http://www.modelt.org

assembly line, 19
belt, 19
Bryant, Clara, 9
buy, 15
car, 11, 13, 15, 17, 19, 21
company, 21
Detroit, 7
engine, 7, 11
factory, 13, 17, 19
farm, 5

Ford Motor Company, 13, 15
gasoline, 7, 11
idea, 7, 9, 21
machines, 5
Michigan, 5
Model A, 13
Model T, 15
power, 11
Quadricycle, 11
worker, 13, 19

Word Count: 216
Early-Intervention Level: 17

Editorial Credits
Martha E. H. Rustad, editor; Kia Bielke, cover designer; Kimberly Danger, photo researcher

Photo Credits
Archive, 14, 18
Baldwin H. Ward/Corbis-Bettmann, cover and inset
Henry Ford Museum, 1, 4, 6, 8, 10, 12, 16, 20